Le Corbusier

Villa Savoye
1931

ル・コルビュジエ
サヴォア邸
1931

LC4 Chaise Longue ©Cassina IXC.Ltd.,

Le Corbusier
Villa Savoye

Photos : Kazuyoshi Miyamoto Text: Yoshiyuki Yamana

目　次

◇住宅写真	4-29
◇図面	38-43
◇ディティール、スケッチ	34-37,52,55
◇「機械」美学としてのサヴォア邸	
パリ郊外と第一機械時代	30
広大な草原に建つ	32
建築的散策	44
最もル・コルビュジエらしい作品	54
「住む機械」と規格化の美学	56
「白の時代」の建築言語	60
リスキーな施主ピエール・サヴォア	60
第一機械時代の最終章、サヴォア邸	62

Contents

◇Photos of the Villa Savoye	4-29
◇Drawings	38-43
◇Details,Sketches	34-37,52,55
◇Villa Savoye and the Art of the "Machine"	
The Parisian Rural and the First Machine Age	31
Built in a Vast Meadow	33
Promenade Architecturale	45
A Representative Work for Le Corbusier	54
"Machine for Living" and Art of the Standardization	57
The Architectural Lingo of the "White Period"	61
Pierre Savoye, the risky client	61
Villa Savoye, the Last Chapter of the First Age Machine	63

サヴォア邸の前奏曲となる門番（庭園管理）小屋の脇から敷地に入り、木々の間を抜けた先に現れる邸宅（南ファサード）。
ピロティの柱の間を通り抜ける自動車通路。自動車は向かって右側よりアプローチする。
写真奥に向かって、小高い丘は傾斜しセーヌ川へ至る。（敷地に隣接するル・コルビュジエ高校の校舎が左側に見える。1958年、校舎増築のために荒廃していたサヴォア邸は取壊しの危機に瀕する。）

The Villa Savoye appears between the trees as one enters the site after passing the guard's house, which in itself is like an introduction to the residence.
The car passage runs between the pilotis. The car approaches from the right side. Moving towards the back of the picture, the low hill inclines slowly towards the Seine River. (On the left, one can see the Le Corbusier high school located on the adjacent site. The abandoned Villa Savoye was endangered of demolition in 1958 with plans for extension of the school.)

▲ 北ファサード
1階：中心軸上にエントランス。2階：北東側（写真右）からキッチン（1ベイ）そして居間（3ベイ）の「水平連続窓」。3階：ソラリウムを囲い込む自立壁に穿たれた開口。

North Façade
1st floor: Entrance on the main axis. 2nd floor: "horizontal strip windows" from the northeast side (right of photograph) to the kitchen (1 bay) and the living room (3 bays). 3rd floor: The "Solarium" is enclosed by free standing walls with pierced openings.

▲ 西ファサード
北のエントランス（写真右側）で客人、主人を降ろした自動車は1階西側に配されたガレージ（緑色の引戸の内側）で待機する。

West Façade
Guests and masters were dropped off at the north entrance (right of photograph) and the cars were the parked at the garage at the west side of the 1st floor (green garage door).

▲ パリからたどり着いた自動車は、ピロティの玄関ホールへと向かう。

Guests in cars visiting from Paris move towards the entrance hall under the pilotis.

▲ 2階部分のスチールサッシの水平連続窓内側は「アブリ（あずまや）」と名付けられた半屋外空間。1階部分の緑色壁の内側は客用アパート（計画案においては運転士用の居住スペース）。この客用アパートのバスルームの開口が見える。（外部のみからのアクセス）。

On the 2nd floor, there is a half outdoor space named the "Abri" inside of the horizontal strip windows with the steel sash. The inside of the green wall on the first floor is an apartment for guests (During design, it was intended as a living space for the driver). The opening of the guest bathroom can be seen here. (access from the exterior).

▲ 西側ピロティ部。右側の緑色に彩色が施された壁の内側は自動車用ガレージ（3台分）。自動車通行部分は小砂利敷。エントランス周りを除いて外部天井は無梁スラブ。

Pilotis on the west side. Behind the green partition is the parking garage (3 cars). The car passage is laid with fine gravel. Excluding the surrounding of the entrance area, external roofs are beamless slabs.

▲エントランスホール。玄関扉から住居階へと上がる「スロープ」は、昇降する装置である「回り階段」と直交に配されている。外部からは主軸線上の丸柱からの梁に沿ってエントランスへと向かう。玄関両脇で二本の柱に置き換わり門型を形成する。門型を潜るように訪問者はスロープへと向かう。向きと柱によって、「回り階段」は訪問者の使用を拒絶しているようでもある。

Entrance hall. "Slope" ascending from the entrance door to the dwelling floor is distributed perpendicular to the "Circular stairway" which is the main device connecting the two floors. From the exterior, one enters the hall by following the beam extended from the pillar on the main axis. Two pillars frame the entrance as a gate leading the visitors to the slope. In a sense, the placement of the "Circular stairway" also suggests an intention to discourage its use.

▲ ソラリウム（屋上）、家人の生活の場（2階）、エントランスホール（1階）と、地下に掘り込まれたカーブ（地下倉庫）を連結する「回り階段」。当初の計画案でサービス（使用人）用に計画されたこの階段は、実現案において、訪問客も使用できるような階段となり、「建築的プロムナード」において欠かせない要素となった。

Circular stairway that connects the "Solarium" (rooftop), family dwelling (2nd floor), entrance hall (1st floor) and the "cave", (underground storage). This staircase was originally planned as a service stair for the servants, but was finally incorporated in the final design, and became for use for the guests as well.
An indispensable element of the Architectural Promenade.

▲ 2階部分へ至るスロープ。内部空間で展開される建築的プロムナード。スロープ西の「空中庭園」から、多くの午後の光が注がれ、スロープ右側の白壁に反射し、地中海的な世界が展開される。

Slope leading to the 2nd floor. Architectural promenade as displayed by the internal space. From the west of the slope, a large amount of light shines in from the suspended garden, and is reflected on the right side wall, giving this space a feeling of a Mediterranean sanctuary.

▲ 大広間より大ガラス越しに、空中庭園を見る。古典的ヴィラ式建築における、パーティーを行う大広間とテラスの関係を空中庭園を挿入することにより組み換えた。
それにより、水平連続窓越しに見える風景と切り取られた空を楽しめるようになり、新たなヴェルヴェデール（見晴らしテラス）が創りだされた。

The suspended garden is seen from a large glass opening from the large hall. As in the architecture of classic villas, the relation sought between the large hall and the terrace is replaced with one with a suspended garden. As a result, one was able to enjoy the scenery by glazing through a horizontal strip windows, and relive the experience of the Belvedere.

◀ 「回り階段」の2階部分。奥のスロープを介して「ジャルダン・サスペンデュ（空中庭園）」が見える。

Circular stairway view from the second floor. The "Jardin Suspendu (suspended garden)" is seen from the inside of the slope.

11

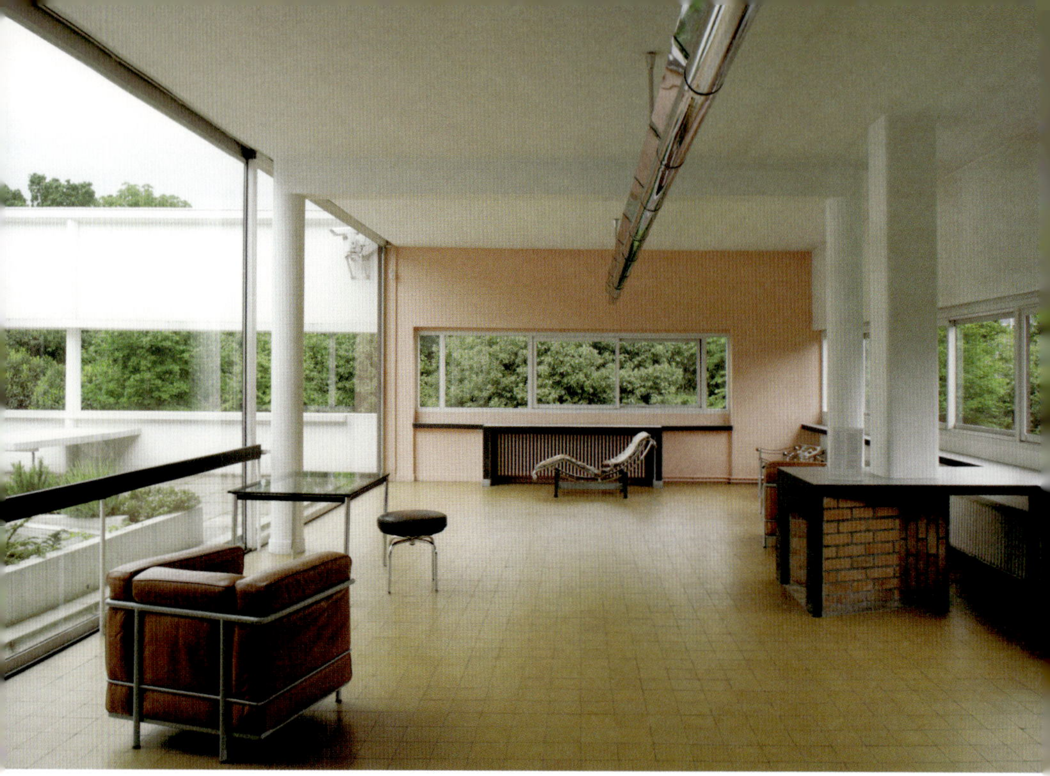

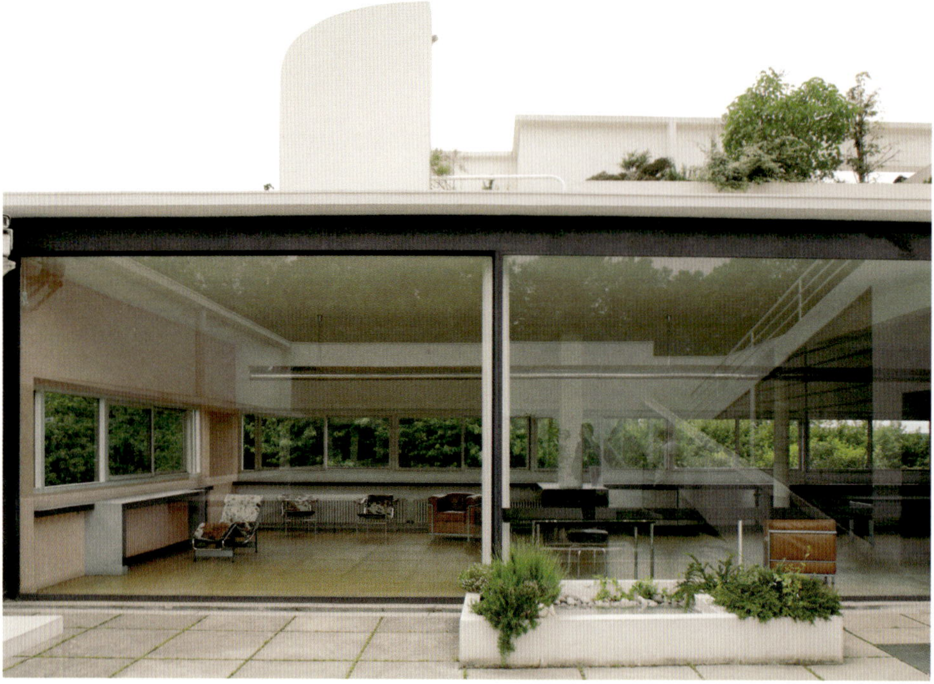

広間（西側を向く）　右手に耐火煉瓦積み暖炉が見える。暖炉の煙突は屋上へと貫く。

The fire proof brick fireplace is seen on the right of the hall (facing west). The chimney of the fireplace is channeled out to the rooftop.

空中庭園と広間を仕切る大ガラス引戸。写真左手の大ガラスの1枚サッシュが右手に引かれる。ル・コルビュジェの従兄弟で協働者であったピエール・ジャンヌレによるメカニカルな検討図面が残されている。

Large glass door that divides the suspended garden and the hall. The sash of the large glass partition on the left of the picture can be slid to the right. A drawing examining the mechanical details drawn by Pierre Jeanerret, Le Corbusier's cousin and partner, still remains.

2階廊下から広間へのガラス扉のル・コルビュジェが幾つかの住宅で使っていた既製品握手。

Detail of the type of ready-made handle used by Le Corbusier in a few of his houses. This one is on the door dividing the 2nd floor corridor to the hall.

▶ 3階部分へと向かう「回り階段」。階段のサービス機能という計画当初の目的は階ごとを「素早く」移動するというものであった。奥（写真右手）に「空中庭園」へと開く扉が見える。写真左側が寝室等のプライベートゾーン。右奥側がパーティなどを行う広間部分。

View of the circular stairway rising up towards the 3rd floor. The original functional purpose of the staircase was to allow for swift circulation between the floors. View of the door that opens to the suspended garden (right of the photograph). The left side of the photograph is the private zone hosting the bedrooms. The right side is the part of the hall where parties were held.

▶ 2階L字型平面の交差部より東側ウイング（プライベートゾーン）の南側を見る。主人寝室が奥に見える。「回り階段」向かいに客用寝室（写真左手）の扉が見える。

The south side of the east wing (private zone) is seen from the intersection part of the 2nd floor L-shaped plan. The master bedroom is seen in the back. The door of the guestroom (left hand of the photograph) is seen opposite of the circular stairway.

▶ 息子用寝室へと向かう廊下。青く彩色の施された壁と寝室入口前のトップライトにより垂直性の強い空間が強調されている。

Passage leading towards the son's bedroom. This space with a strong verticality is dramatized with a blue wall and a skylight in front of the bedroom.

17

▲ 2階の南東コーナーに配された息子用寝室。写真右にあるワードローブの手前にベッドが置かれていた。裏側が書斎。書斎は南側に位置し、息子は水平連続窓から客人のアプローチを窺うことが出来た。

The son's bedroom is located at the southeast corner of the 2nd floor. In front of the wardrobe on the right of the photograph, is placed a bed. On the other side, there is a study. The study was located on the south, so that the son was able to look out of the horizontal strip windows, and see the guests approach.

▲ 息子用寝室。東側の水平連続窓。奥の赤色の彩色が施された壁の裏側が主人用バスルーム。

Son's bedroom. The horizontal strip windows on the east side. Behind the red wall was the master's bathroom.

18

息子用バスルーム。浴槽の形に添った曲面壁。
Son's bathroom. The curvacious wall molding the shape of the bathtub.

「家事設備」と名付けられたワードローブ、棚は、ふたつの場を区切る空間構成要素。右側は寝室となり、左側は書斎となっている。
Wardrobes and shelves were named "household equipments" as they also served the purpose of dividing two spaces. The right side is the bedroom and the left is the study.

▲ 2階の北東に位置するキッチン

チャーチ邸（1927）のキッチンが気に入ったサヴォア婦人は、単なる週末用調理場ではなく、最新設備の整った機能的なキッチンを求めた。多くの訪問客にも応えられるように配膳室と共にチャーチ邸よりも大きなスペースが要求された。写真左側はハッチを兼備えた「機能的」食器棚。棚の引戸はアルミ板。この棚の裏側が配膳室。写真手前側には冷蔵庫スペース、棚の並びには「生ごみ受」（配膳室の裏側は「ほうき入」）、扉を介してサービスバルコニーがある。

The kitchen located on the northeast of the 2nd floor. Mrs. Savoye who really liked the design of the kitchen at the Villa Church (1927) requested a functional kitchen where it would not become just a place for cooking on the weekend, but rather had to be equipped with the latest in kitchenware. A space wider than the Villa Church was demanded including a pantry for the servant, so that it would be able to serve a large number of guests. On the left side of the photograph is a "functional" tableware shelf equipped with hatches. The doors of the shelf are made of aluminum panels. The other side of this shelf is the butler's pantry. At the front of the photograph is a space for the refrigerator, in row with the shelf is the garbage disposal (in the back of the pantry is the broom storage), and behind the door is the service balcony.

▶ ブドワ（婦人用小サロン・私室）。主寝室を経由して至る。窓を介して2階の「空中庭園」の目隠し用の植栽が見える。写真右手が主寝室。左手が扉を介して外部である「アブリ」へ出られる。部屋の中心に円形の暖炉が計画されていた。

Boudoir (small salon and private space for the women). Arriving via the master bedroom. By the window there are plants placed for the screening of the suspended garden on the 2nd floor. On the right of the photograph is the master bedroom. The door on the left hand side opens up to the exterior and leads one into the "Abri". At the center of the room, a round shaped fireplace had been planned.

◀ 調理台は7×22cmの白磁器質タイルが貼られている。調理台と一体化した当時としては画期的であったビィルトインシンク。セーヌ川へと至る眺望を楽しみながら、洗い物を行う。

White porcelain tiles of 7×22cm were laid for the kitchen counter. At that time, the built-in sink in counter was an innovation in itself. One was able to do the dishes while looking out the panorama of the Seine River.

メインバスルーム。キッチン同様（7×22cm）の白磁器質タイルが貼られている。トップライトからの光に照らし出された、寝椅子に張られたグレーのガラスタイルとバスタブのトルコブルーのガラスタイル（5×5cm）の対比が印象的である。奥にトイレ、キャビネットに入る黒茶色の扉が見える。

The main bathroom. The white porcelain tile similar to the ones used for the kitchen (7×22cm) was used. Light shining through the skylight dawns a sparkle to the different tile qualities such as the grey glass tiles used on the chaise longue and the turkish blue tiles used for the bathtub (5×5cm). At the end of the room, there is the toilet, and one can also see the dark brown cabinet door.

バスルームに設けられたトップライト下の磁器製の洗面器とビデ。グレーに彩色が施された丸柱に洗面用照明がある。構造体である柱と梁から間仕切り壁（パロワ）が独立していることがわかる。

The porcelain sink and bidet under the skylight. On the grey pillar, there is a light fixture for the sink. The partition wall (paroi) is independent from the structural pillars and beam.

▲ ビルトインによるバスタブ。写真左に水栓が見える。

Built-in bathtub. The plughole is seen on the left of the photograph.

両親用寝室から見たバスルーム（写真左）。写真右手奥行き方向の壁に外部スロープの断面が見える。高さ2.26mのワードローブによってドレッシングルームとバスルームが仕切られている。息子用寝室同様に床仕上げは木フローリング。

Bathroom (left of photograph) seen from the master bedroom. On the right of the photograph, one can see the section of the external slope from the wall extended towards the back. The dressing room and the bathroom have been partitioned with the 2.26m high wardrobe. A wood flooring finish was used similarly for the son's bedroom.

▲ 3階のソラリウム（屋上庭園）より2階の空中庭園を見下ろす。フラットルーフの防水の立ち上がりがほとんど取られていなかったことがわかる。これが、その後さまざまな問題を引き起こす。

Looking down to the 2nd floor suspended garden from the solarium of the 3rd floor (roof garden). There is hardly an edge for waterproofing for the flat roof. This in fact became the origin of diverse problems.

▲ 1階から2階への内部スロープ、2階から3階への外部スロープ、そして空中庭園を見る。サッシ割りが1階の垂直から水平へと変わる。

View of the external slope connecting the 1st floor to the 2nd floor, external slope connecting the 2nd floor to the 3rd floor, and then the suspended garden. The sash divisions change from a vertical to horizontal pattern.

地上3.5mメートルのところに設定された「空中庭園」。つまり、空から「吊下げられた庭園」。湿気の多いポワッシーの丘の緑を、人工地盤から水平連続窓越しに眺める。奥に見えるのが屋根のついた半屋外空間である「アブリ」。

The height of the suspended garden is at 3.5 meters above ground. In other words "A garden hung from the sky". The green hills of humid Poissy were seen from the artificial floor and through the large horizontal strip window. In the back, there is the roofed part of the semi-exterior "Abri" space.

空中庭園よりスロープを見る。3階の屋上庭園には回り階段のヴォリュームが見える。そのヴォリュームと鉛直方向で連続する回り階段手摺壁がガラス越しに見える。ピュリスム絵画のようである。

The slope seen from the suspended garden. The volume of the circular stairway is seen from the roof garden of the 3rd floor. One can see this staircase, which is perpendicular to the slope volume, through the peering glass. The composition is just like a Purist painting.

▲ スロープを上がりソラリウム（日光浴場）へと至る。スロープ正面にセーヌ川方向を見下ろす開口部がある。

The solarium at the top of the slope. There is an opening that looks down towards the Seine River at the end of the slope.

▲ 自由な間仕切壁（パロワ）によって囲まれた3階ソラリウム。

The 3rd floor solarium contained by the freestanding partition walls (paroi).

▲ 開口部前のテーブルにシャンパングラスを置き、開口部越しのセーヌ川へ続く田園風景を見ながら商談の話でもしたのであろうか。プラントボックスの中の緑と遠景の緑と対比が見れる。

With champagne glasses on the table, we could imagine that they must have been talking business while looking at the pastoral fields extending all the way to the Seine River through these openings. There is also a relational comparison of the vegetation in the planter boxes and the landscape in the background.

▲「回り階段」で1階エントランスホールへと降りる。
Going down to the first floor entrance hall by the circular stairway.

◀ らせん階段のダイナミックな形態には当時、機械文明が加速するイメージと重なり、多くの前衛芸術家たちも関心を寄せた。

At that time, the dynamic shape of the spiral staircase sparked many of the avant-garde artists' interest in its correspondence to the machine age.

▲ スロープによってソラリウムに到達した訪問者は、3階より内部に入り「回り階段」で下階へと降りる。

The visitor who reaches the solarium by ascending the slope to the 3rd floor should move towards the inside and descend via the circular stairway.

「機械」美学としてのサヴォア邸

パリ郊外と第一機械時代

　ローマの歴史的遺産にはかなわないが、パリは21世紀まで連綿と続くそれぞれの時代の「今日の建築」を見ることができる。他の近代都市と同様に、パリとその郊外も、産業革命以降に膨張を続けた。パリの姿の大部分は18世紀から19世紀にかけて作られ、郊外は20世紀にその多くが作られた。サヴォア邸の位置する郊外を通してむしろ20世紀前半、つまり第一機械時代のパリの様相を想像することができる。

　サヴォア邸を訪れるためには、パリの中心であるレ・アール駅から高速地下鉄RER A線（1時間に5,6本）で、デファンス駅などを通過して西へ1時間弱、終点のポワッシー駅で下車する。ポワッシーは治安の良い良質な郊外のひとつである。今では、ブルジョワ層の週末住宅の周りに中産階級の住宅が拡がり、典型的な郊外住宅地となっている。1930年代にポワッシー市にはアメリカのフォード自動車の工場が作られ、現在は、プジョー自動車の工場として稼動している。

　駅からサヴォア邸へは、徒歩で丘を登って25分ほどである。サヴォア邸はフランスの重要文化財に指定されているため、標識を辿れば目的地に到着することができる。少し時間のある方には、セーヌ川沿いの公園を経由しながらサヴォア邸を訪れることをお勧めしたい。

　サヴォア邸訪問の正統派は、やはり自動車での訪問である。パリ市内からは、新凱旋門のあるデファンス地区を抜け、新設のノルマンディー高速道路を使い、20分〜30分でポワッシー市に到着する。高速道路のない当時は、パリから国道13号線、通称ノルマンディー道をセーヌ川に沿って西へ車を走らせたのであろう。

Villa Savoye and the Art of the Machine

The Parisian Rural and the First Machine Age

The city of Paris, although not comparable to the deep historic heritage of Rome, is a witness of the most contemporary architecture of its time up until the 21st century. Much like other modern cities of its time, Paris and its suburbs kept on expanding throughout the Industrial Revolution. The majority of Paris was constructed from the 18th century to the 19th century and most of the suburbs in the 20th century. A walk in the suburbs of the Villa Savoye enables one to imagine what it would have been like in the first half of the 20th century Paris in the First Machine Age.

To visit the Villa Savoye, one must take a high speed train from Les Halles station, RER A line (5-6 trains per hour), pass the La Defense station and continue towards the west, and get off at the Poissy station terminal. Poissy is a safe and comfortable suburb in France. Nowadays, middle class houses are expanding around the Villa Savoye, making it a typical subtopia area. The factory of the American carmaker Ford was built in Poissy city in the 1930's, and it is now operating as a factory for Peugeot.

From the station to the Villa Savoye, it takes about 25 minutes on foot. And since the building itself is listed as a national heritage of France, there are many signs that take you directly to the destination. A recommendation for those who have some extra time, it is recommended that they take a walk in the park along the Seine River, on their way to the villa.

The orthodox way to visit the Villa Savoye would be to visit by car. From the city of Paris, depart the city of La Defense where is located the Arch of Triumph, take the newly constructed Normandy expressway, and you may reach Poissy in about 20-30 minutes. At the time when there wasn't an expressway, from Paris one would have had to take Route 13, commonly known as the Normandy road, and drive west along the Seine River.

広大な草原に建つ

「緩やかなドーム状に盛り上がった広大な草原」にサヴォア邸は建つ。ポワッシーの中心から西へ、乱石積の塀をつたって小高い丘の坂を上って行く。

粗末な門を入ると右手に門番小屋がある。この小屋にも「近代建築の五原則」がほぼ実現され、サヴォア邸のミニチュア版ともいえる。本邸を訪れる前の前奏曲の気分になるが、鉛直性が強すぎて、どことなくプロポーションが悪い。林の中の砂利道を歩く音を聞きながら、しばらく進むと木立が開け、急に明るくなる。

右手に突然、ピロティによって宙に持ち上げられた「白いヴォリューム」が現れる。重苦しいパリの街からサヴォア邸を訪れると、小高い丘の上にそっと置かれたサヴォア邸のヴォリュームの自由さ、軽さに驚かされる。ウィーンの美術史家H・ゼーテルマイヤーが著書『中心の喪失』のなかでサヴォア邸を「地上に舞い降りた宇宙船」と評したことも理解できる。

木立の緑と砂利の白が、視界が開けた後、草原と1階部分の壁の緑とヴォリュームの壁の白に転換する。そのヴォリュームの下へ、ピロティの柱の間を通り抜けて、白い砂利道が周りの緑を切り取るように続く。当時のように左ハンドルの運転で建物の右側から左回りで建物にアクセスすることを想像してほしい。

● 1階天井の梁は構造による論理だけでなく空間の整合性によって架けられている。

The beam in the first floor ceiling is designed by correspondence of spaces, not only by structural rational.

Built in a Vast Meadow

The Villa Savoye was built on a "Vast meadow that rises up in a gradual dome". From the center of Poissy to the west, move along the random masonry wall and climb the slow slope of the small hill.

By entering the shabby door, there is a guard's house. And one would realize that even at the guard's house, the Five Points of Modern Architecture were implemented, and even to say that it is a miniature version of the Villa itself. Although the perpendicular seems to be too strong, and the ratio is somehow unbalanced, it exerts the feeling of a prelude introducing the entrance to the villa. Walking for a while through the grove on the rocky road, and the woods suddenly open up.

There appears on the right hand side a "white volume" lifted on pilotis. Visitors coming from gloomy Paris are always overwhelmed by the freedom and the lightness of the Villa Savoye quietly sitting on the low hill. Viennese art historian H.Zatelmeyer criticized the building in his book "Verlust der Mitte" by calling it a "Spaceship that landed and dancing on the ground".

The view of the green grove and the white gravel converts smoothly to the green of the plantations and the white walls of the building. Moving towards the under part of the volume, and passing through the piloti pillars, the white graveled path continues and surround the green plantations. As at that time, steering on the left side of the wheel, one can imagine accessing the building by running left on the right side of the building.

門番小屋。「近代建築の五原則」がほぼ実現されている。

Guard's house. Five Points of Modern Architecture practically achieved.

Detail - 1

• 1階天井は基本的に無梁版スラブである。外部に接しているところは外断熱となり、内側と比べると相対的に天井が下がっている。これによりサッシュの上端が天井にのみこまれている。内部は直天。サッシュは内側が白、外側が黒く塗られている。

The first floor's ceiling is principally a beam-less slab. The part which is connected to the outside becomes an outer insulation and by comparing the two sides, the ceiling here is much lower than the side of the interior. The ceiling is completely framed by the sash. The inside is directly opened to the sky. The inside of the sash is painted white, while the exterior is painted black.

水平連続窓のスチールサッシまわり。
1930年代初頭はフランスにおいてさまざまなスチールサッシの特許が開発された。当時、主に工場に使用されていたスチールサッシをヴィラ（邸宅）建築に大胆に用いたことは異例なことであった。上部に壁厚を利用したカーテンボックスが見える。内側開口枠はスチールの厚さを考慮した木製枠となっている。

Around the steel sash of horizontal strip windows. Patents of a variety of steel sashes were developed in France in the 1930's. However, the use of steel sashes mainly developed for factory use in the design of villa residences was a gutsy incentive. The curtain box using the thickness of the wall is seen on the top. On the inside of the opening, a wooden material taking in consideration the texture of the steel is used.

35

Detail - 2

2階スロープ部分の水平フィックスサッシュ。サッシュ内側には、結露受けがコンクリートによって造られている。最下部へは結露抜きがある（写真上部）。

The horizontal fixed sash on 2nd floor slope. On the inside of the sash, the dew receptor is made out of concrete. At the lowest part, there is a dew drain. (upper part of the photograph).

外部と空中庭園の間にある水平開口。サッシュはない。水平ハンチが開口部に影をつくりメリハリをつける。柱も外部からの見え方を考慮して紡錘形断面をしている。

Horizontal opening between the exterior and suspended garden. There is no sash. The horizontal haunch casts a shadow at the opening, and there is a cast roof. The form of the pillars were also designed to reflect the views from the exterior, therefore were sculpted in a spindle-shaped.

(Photos:©Yoshiyuki Yamana P32-37)

平面図／Floor plans

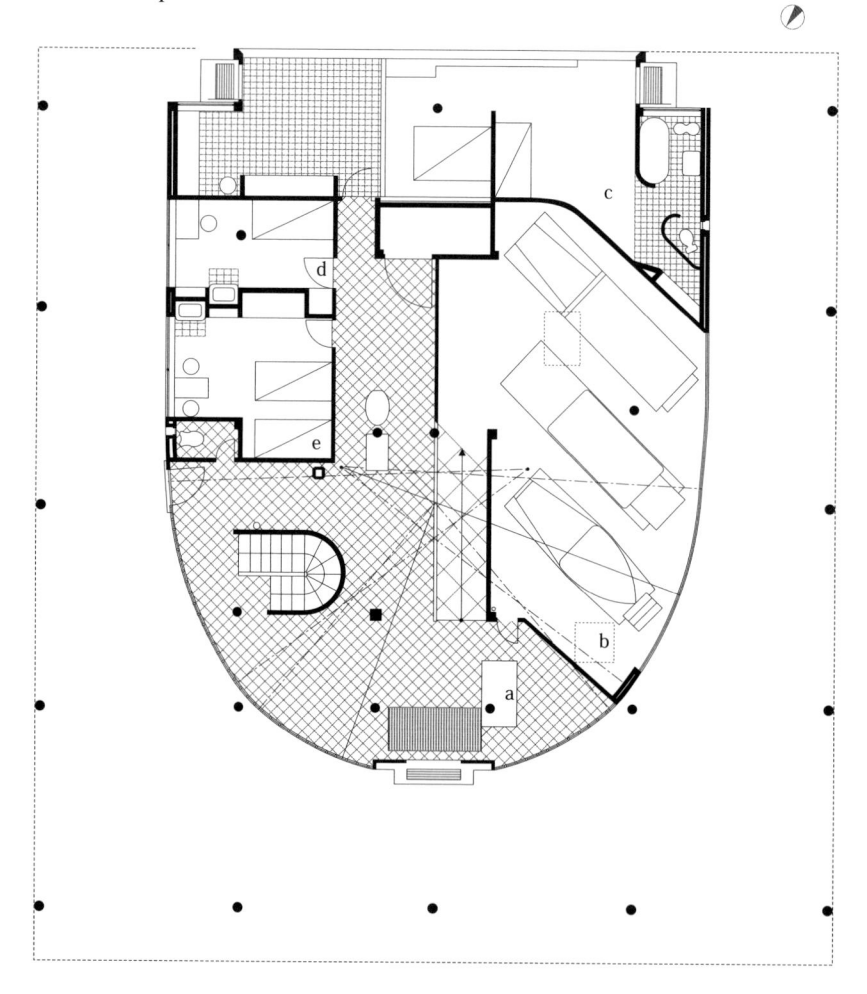

1/200

1階（左頁）2階（右頁）の平面図。構造体である柱より間仕切り（壁）がまったく自由となっている。場所によっては、柱さえも1階と2階で一致していないところがある。

1st floor plan (left page) and 2nd floor plan (right page). The partition walls are absolutely freestanding from the pillars. Even the positioning of the pillars does not necessarily correspond to the grid of the 1st floor and 2nd floor.

a. エントランスホール　b. ガレージ　c. ゲスト用ルーム（運転手用ルーム）d. 使用人寝室1　e. 使用人寝室2

a.Entrance hall b.Garage c.Guest room (Driver's room) d.Servant's room 1 e.Servant's room 2

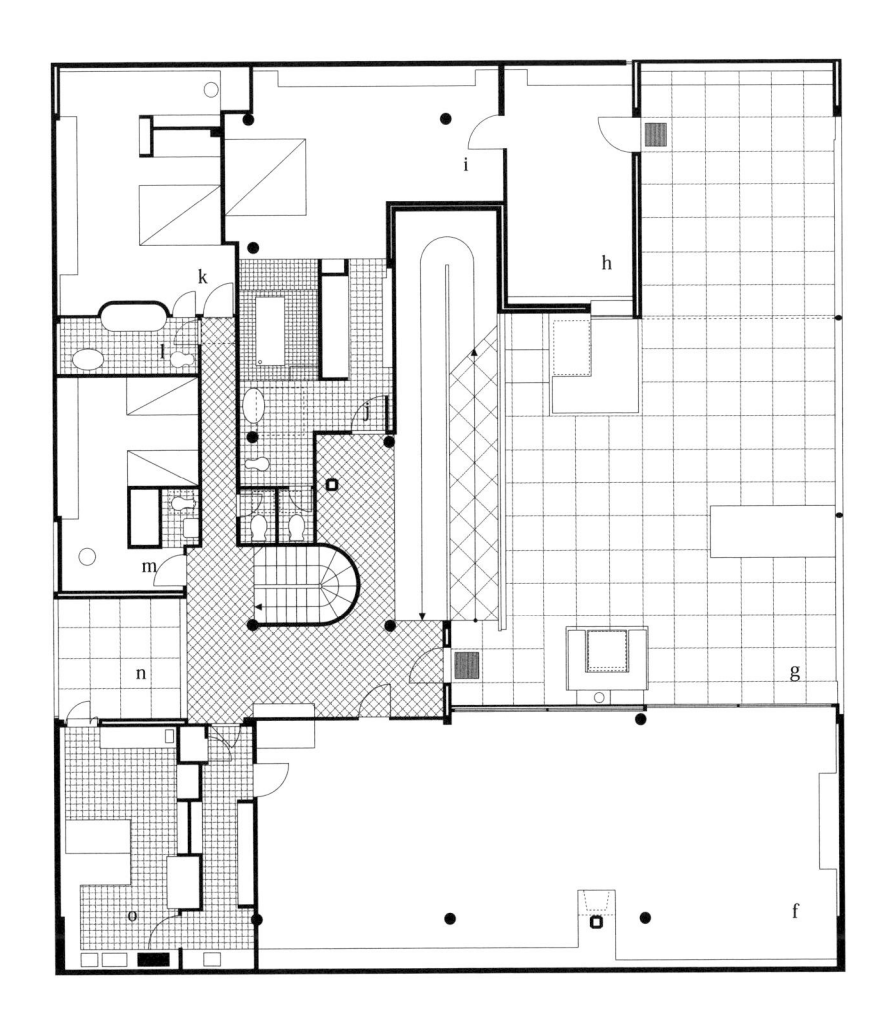

f. 居間　g. テラス（空中庭園）h. ブドワ（婦人用サロン）i. 主寝室　j. バスルーム　k. 息子用寝室　l. バスルーム　m. ゲスト用寝室　n. サービス用テラス　o. キッチン

f.Living room g.Terrace (Suspended garden) h.Boudoir (Women's room) i.Master bedroom j.Bathroom k.Son's room l.Bathroom m.Guest room n.Service terrace o.Kitchen

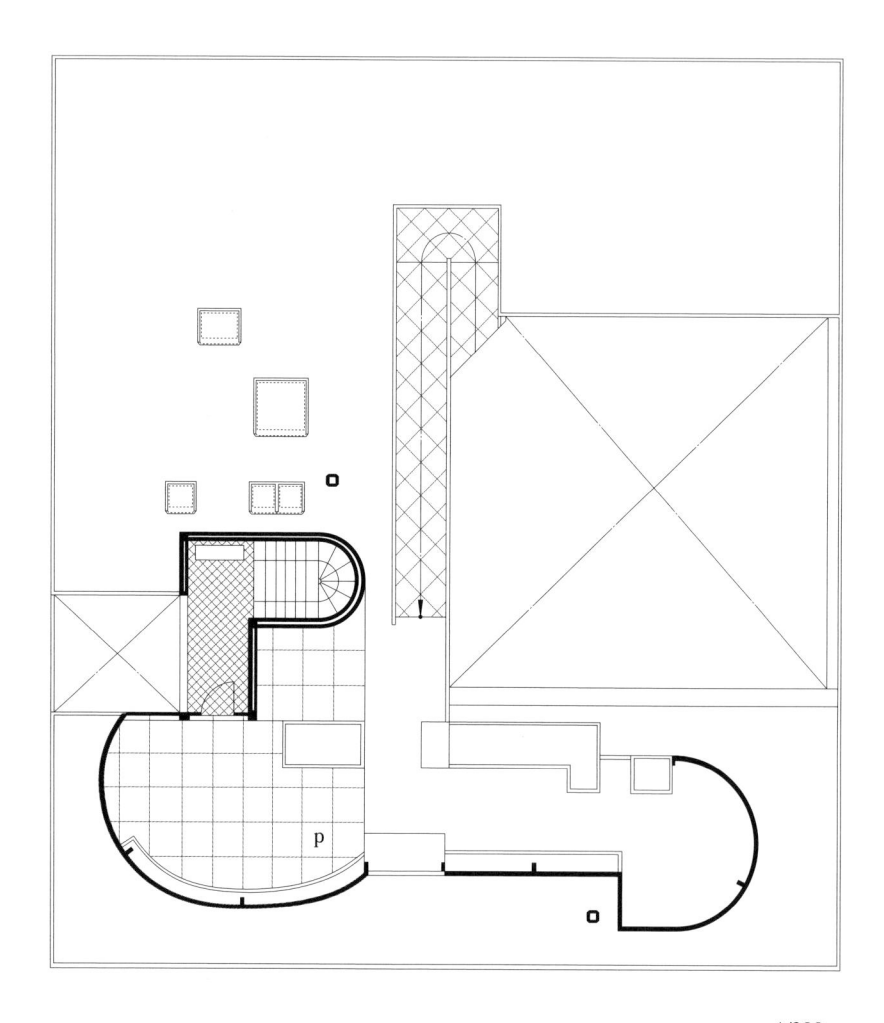

1/200

● 3階平面図。セーヌ川から吹き上げる風を遮るために壁が設けられた。造形的な曲面壁は、ピュリスム絵画のようでもある。

3rd floor plan. To interrupt the wind blown up from the Seine River, a wall was placed here. Its curvaceous wall is reminiscent of a Purist painting.

p. ソラリウム（日光浴場）
p.Solarium (Sunbathing place)

透視図／Axonometric Perspective

- 「自由な平面」とは、お互いの平面を拘束しあわないことである。メゾン・ドミノで提示されたフレーム構造によって提案された。

  The idea behind the "free plan" is to be able to detach two floor plans from each other. It was developed with the design of the framework of the Maison Domino.

断面図／Section Plan

- 2階に位置するキュービックな主階をスロープが突き抜けている。

  The slope pierces through the cubic main floor located on the second floor.

North-South   1/200

41

立面図／Elevation

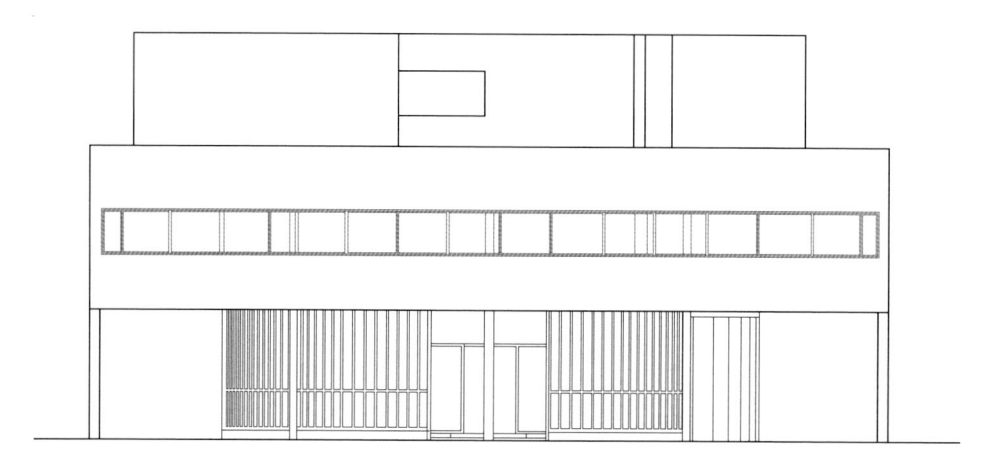

North

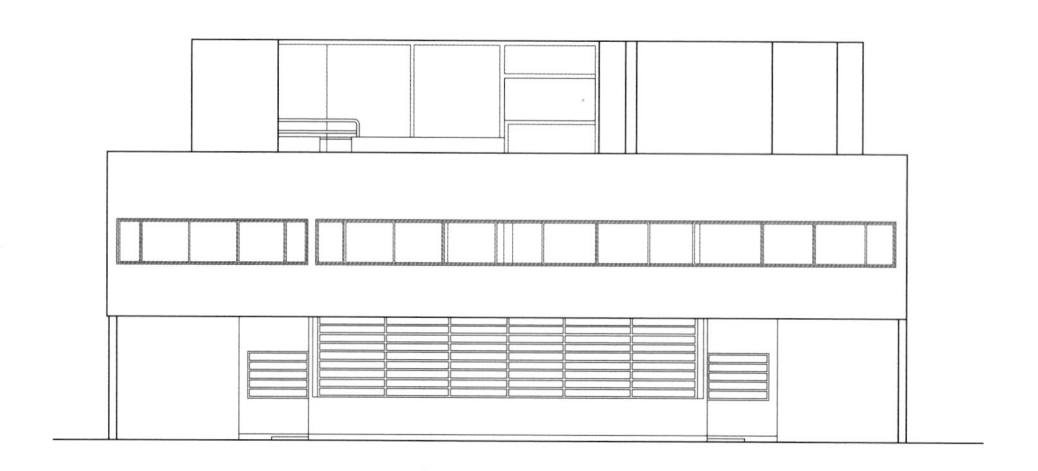

South

● 五原則の最終項目として提案された「自由な立面」は、第一項目「ピロティ」と第二項目「屋上庭園」の間で展開された「自由な平面」の結果としてあらわれる。

The "free façade" proposed as the final item of the five points appears as a result of the "free plan" developed between the first item the "piloti" and the second item the "roof garden".

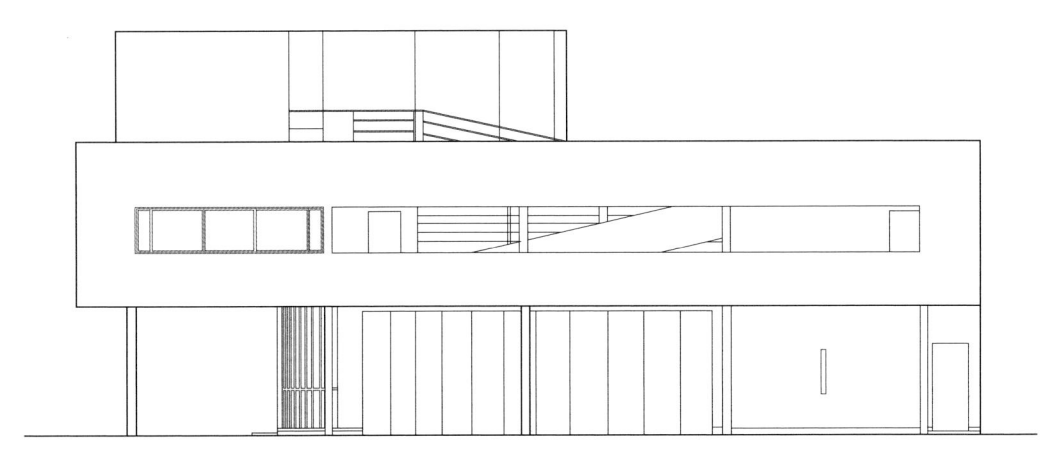

West

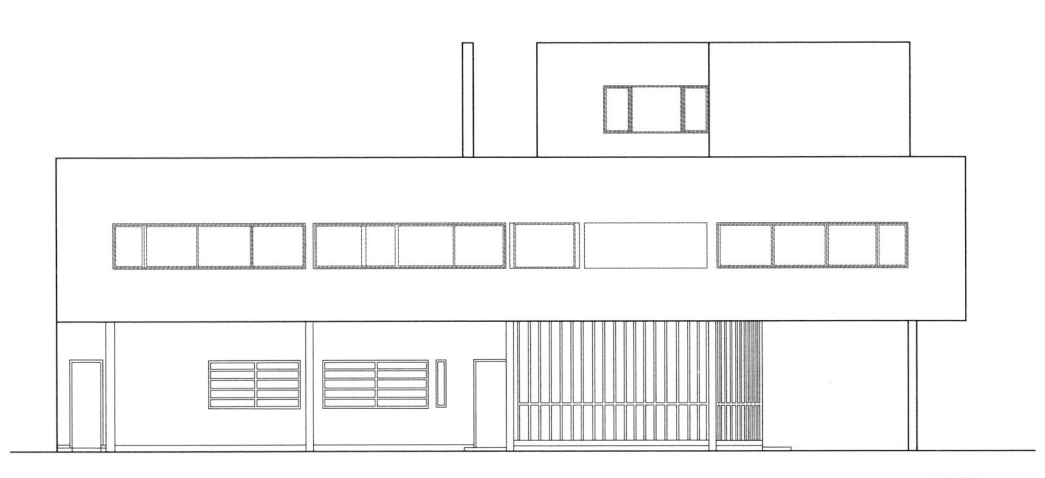

East

1/200

建築的散策

エントランスホール

　1階のエントランス周りの奇妙な馬蹄形は、自動車の回転軌跡から編み出されたもので、半円形ではない。エントランスで客人、主人を下ろした後、方向転換することなく、そのまま建物内にしつらえられたガレージに入れるか、そのまま建物の下を回って帰途につく。

　降りた客人は、上方でピロティの柱から伸びる梁を辿りながら、エントランスの扉へと導かれる。黒いスチールドアを開け、中に入ると辿ってきた梁はT字型になり、2本の柱で受けられる。この2本の柱とそれらを繋ぐ梁による門型を潜り抜け、客人は上方からの自然光によって、自然とスロープへと導かれる。

　60平米ほどのエントランスホールには、スロープ以外に、下階のカーヴ（ワインなどの貯蔵庫）と上階に繋がる回り階段がある。このエントランス周りを見渡すと、柱は角柱、丸柱と注意深く使い分けられていることがわかる。そのほか、柱と一体となったテーブル、工業化社会を象徴したような既製品の洗面台などがこの空間に配置されている。

　1階には住むための空間はほとんどない。車3台分のカーポートから直接、エントランスに入れるが、運転手用のアパートは、外部西側からアクセスするようになっている。その他にリネン室などの諸設備のほか、使用人たちの部屋がふたつある。

スロープによって上の階へ

　スロープによって建築体験の気分が高まる。ル・コルビュジエは「建築的プロムナード」をアラブ的空間と呼んでいた。バロック建築のように、紙の上で理論的に点と点から展開されるものとは全く違い、アラブ的空間は足で感じ、移動することにより建築が表現しようとしているものを知ることができると指摘している。そして、この「建築的プロムナード」を実現すべくサヴォア邸では、予期しない眺めや意外な発見に満ちた空間の連続が展開されている。

　スロープを折り返して昇りきると、ピアノ・ノービレ（主階）[※1]である2階に到達する。2階の平面配置は1階の左右対称性の強い構成と異なり、空中庭園（ジャルダン・サスペンデュ）を

玄関脇にある洗面器。ル・コルビュジエの建築の多くにみられる特徴のひとつで、衛生思想を反映している。
Sink at the side of the entrance. A characteristic of many of Le Corbusier's architecture is its sensibility to hygiene.

Promenade Architecturale

Entrance Hall

A strange horseshoe shaped area around the entrance of the first floor is inspired by the projection of the turning of a car, which is in fact not a half circle. This design allows the driver of the vehicle to enter the garage right after dropping off the passengers, or turn out to the exit without having to turn the vehicle around.

The guest, after getting off the car, is led to the entrance door by following the beam expanding from the upper piloti. By opening a steel door, and entering the inside, the beam that was extended from the exterior becomes a T-section beam, supported by two columns. These two columns and the beam that they support become a gate that welcomes the guest, at the same time attracted by a natural light from the above, leading them to nature through slope.

In the entry hall measuring around 60 square meters, other than the slope, there is a connecting circular staircase that links the wine cellar to the upper floor. If carefully observed, one realizes that the usage of square and round pillars was also carefully thought out. Additionally, one also realizes that objects such as the pillar-table unit and ready-made products are very reminiscent of the society of industrialization.

There is little space for living on the first floor. The 3-car parking lot connects directly to the entrance, but the apartment reserved for the driver must be accessed externally on the west side. Additionally, there are two servant rooms and other functional rooms such as the linen room.

Going to the Upper Floor on the Slope

The feeling of an architectural experience is enhanced by using the slope. Le Corbusier called the "Architectural promenade" an Arabic space. Le Corbusier remarked that, like Baroque architecture, unlike merely connecting two points, an Arabic space is felt with the feet, and one becomes aware of the architectural expression while at the same time moving. To achieve this "Architectural promenade", the continuousness of the spaces stringed through with unanticipated views and unexpected discoveries make up the design of the Villa Savoye.

As one turns the slope, one reaches the Piano Nobile[*1] (main floor) on the second level. The plan of the second floor, unlike the strong symmetry of the first floor, is arranged in an L shape, as to surround a suspended garden (jardin suspendu). Using the circular

---

[*1] ピアノ・ノービレ
古典的なルネッサンス建築スタイルの邸宅における2階（主階）のことをいう。2階に主室（リビング、ダイニングルーム、ベッドルームなど）があり、その上下階と比較すると床面積が広いだけではなく天井も高い。
Piano Nobile
The second floor in a Classical Renaissance style for residential architecture (main floor) Main rooms on this floor are the living room, dining room, and bedroom, and in comparison with the lower and upper floors, it is not only wider in area but also more generous in ceiling height.

囲むようにL字型に構成されている。回り階段の位置を基点に南北方向の東側を寝室などのプライベートゾーン、東西軸の北側に広間／ダイニングルームなどパブリックゾーンが配置されている。スロープはこのL字の交点部分に達し、正面にこの住宅で唯一のガラス扉がある。この扉が開き、客人はサロンに案内されるのである。

ピアノ・ノービレの週末生活

　サヴォア邸は週末住宅である。金曜日の夕方にパリを離れ、土曜日の午後に友人や親戚、ビジネスのパートナーなどを招待して、週末生活を楽しむ。週末のパーティーは上流社会に限らず、現在でもフランスで日常的に行なわれている生活パターンである。この週末とヴァカンスのためにフランス人は働いていると言っても過言ではない。

　この広間で食事をするが、アペリティフ（食前酒）からはじまる晩餐は、少なくとも3～4時間ほどかかるのが普通である。パリは緯度が高く標準時も日本より遅く設定しているため、5月から10月までは、日の入りが20時から23時位である。ゆっくりと沈んでゆく太陽の光のもとで、アペリティフをもって広間から出て、西側の空中庭園で楽しみながら、3階の屋上庭園まで昇り、商談の話や家族の話をしていたのであろう。

　空中庭園を挟んで広間と反対側に、ブドワと呼ばれる婦人用小サロンがある。ここは主寝室と隣り合っているが、ここはサヴォア婦人のプライベートルームである。パーティーには商談のパートナーであれ、カップルで訪問することが常識である。男たちが3階のソラリウムに昇って、テーブルに腰を掛け、セーヌ川へ続く田園風景でも見ながら商談の話をしているのを、このブドワに唯一付けられた正方形の開口部から、額縁越しに、夫人同士で眺め、笑いながらカード遊びでも楽しんでいたのであろうか。

　空中庭園の一角、ブドワに隣接してアブリと呼ばれる半屋外空間がある。南西のコーナーにあるが、壁の一方にはスチールサッシュが入り、もう一方の西側は単なる開口になっているという不思議な場所だ。ここからサロン側を見る形で、左側に開口越しに広大な草原の水平線を、正面に大ガラス越しに広間を、右側にスロープによって上昇して行く空間を、設計中、ル・コルビュジエは透視図で何度もスケッチを繰り返した。このシー

空中庭園のアブリ。
Abri of the suspended garden.

staircase as the point of reference, the east side of the north-south axis consists of the private zone with the bedrooms; the northern side of the east-west axis consists of the public zone with the hall and dining room. The slope ends at the intersection of this L-shaped area, and right in front is placed the only glass door in the house. By opening this door, one is welcomed into the "salon" living space.

Piano Nobile and the Weekend Life

The Villa Savoye is a house for the weekend. The owners leave Paris on the Friday evening, and on Saturday afternoon, friends, family and business partners are invited to enjoy a weekend of fun at the house. The weekend party was not a lifestyle limited to only the high society, and even today is a lifestyle practiced in France. It would not be an exaggeration to say that the French work all week to party and go on vacation on the weekends.

The dinner at the hall would usually start with an aperitif and would generally last for 3-4 hours. The latitude of Paris is higher than that of Japan; therefore, the sunset is also later, ranging usually from 8pm to 11pm between May and October. With the slowly dimming sunset as a backdrop, the aperitif is brought out from the hall, while enjoying the delicacies from the suspended garden on the west side. One can also enjoy a splendid conversation about business or family while escalating the slope to the third floor roof garden.

On the other side of the suspended garden, opposite of the salon, is a small hall space for the ladies called the "boudoir". Although the purpose of the parties was mostly for business, it was common mannerism to attend as a couple. The men would go up to the third floor "solarium", have a seat at the table and talk business while enjoying the view of the Seine River and the pastoral landscapes. At the same time, there is an opening that looks into the "boudoir" where they can peek to see their wives, while playing cards and having a good laugh.

In one corner of the suspended garden, there is a semi-outdoor space called the "abri" which is connected to the "boudoir". Located on the south-west corner, one opening is framed with a steel sash, but on the west side, there is a mysterious frameless opening. From here one is placed to look into the salon, while through the opening, different views are displayed: through the opening on the left, one can see the horizon of the meadow, while on the front glass is the hall, and on the right is the view of the rising slope; a design that Le Corbusier had repeatedly sketched in axonometric. This scene might have been the most important for Le Corbusier. On the wall on the west side, there is a peek opening, and by looking inside one can really

ンガ・ルコルビュジエにとって一番重要なものであったのであろう。西側の壁に穿たれた開口に纏わる、台形の水平ハンチ、紡錘形をした柱の断面など、構造上の合理性のうえに、内側からの見え方と同時に、外側から、この開口部越しに、どのように見えるかが詳細に検討されたことが窺える。

寝室とバスルーム

　2階には主寝室、ゲスト用寝室、息子用寝室といった、もうひとつの意味で住宅において最も重要なものがある。L字型平面のプライベートゾーンにこれらはあるが、このゾーンも縦にふたつのエリアに分かれる。東側にあるのが、息子の書斎兼寝室、ここの内側からもダイレクトにアクセスできるバスルーム、そしてゲスト用寝室である。（竣工当時、サヴォア夫妻の息子は結婚前の青年で、週末になるとよく彼女が遊びに来ては、このゲストルームに泊まっていたらしい。）これらには幅の狭い、垂直性の強い廊下でアプローチすることになるが、青く彩色の施された廊下の奥には、トップライトからの自然光が差し込み、地中海的な世界を作り出している。

　もうひとつのエリアには、主寝室と、サヴォア邸のクライマックスのひとつであるトップライトによる自然光で満たされたバスルームがある。ここには洗面台、ビデなどの衛生機器も置かれ自然光に照らし出されている。メインのシーンは水色のガラスモザイクタイルによって張られたバスタブと、当時、シャルロット・ペリアン[※2]とデザインしていたシェーズロングのプロトタイプとほぼ同じ断面を持つガラスモザイクタイル張りの寝椅子に自然光が射していることであろう。白の磁器質タイル

[※2] シャルロット・ペリアン
建築家、デザイナー。フランス生まれ。（1903-1999）
パリの装飾美術中央連合学校（エコールUCAD）卒業後、1927年サロン・ドートンヌに「屋根裏のバー」を出展し、大反響を巻き起こす。この作品がきっかけで、コルビジェのアトリエへ入る。ル・コルビュジェ、ピエール・ジャンヌレと共に、シェーズロングを始め、数々の名作を世に送り出した。

Charlotte Perriand
Architect and designer. Born in France (1903-1999)
After graduating from UCAD in Paris, she exhibited "Bar in the attic" at the salon Dortonnu in 1927, gained popularity from then on. Thanks to this project, she joined Le Corbusier's atelier. A lot of masterpieces including the "Chaise Longue" traveled around the world with Le Corbusier and Pierre de Jeanerret.

水平連続窓の前に置かれているシェーズロングLC4。全体を支える金属パイプの曲線と身体の線にあわせて曲げられた線との対比が印象的。

The "Chaise Longue" LC4 put in front of the ribbon window. View of the curvaceous lines of the support pipes, and the line of the seductive body.

understand the constructional rationality, such as the trapezoidal horizontal haunch and the section of the spindle-shaped columns, also that the opening was meant to be looked through both from the interior and exterior.

The Bedroom and Bathroom

On the second floor, there is the master bedroom, guestroom, son's room, and is another important component of the house. While these are located in the L-shaped private zone, it is additionally divided into 2 zones in itself. On the east side, there is the son's bedroom and study, which in the back can access the bathroom and the guestroom. (It is told that during construction that Savoye's son was still single, but would bring his girlfriend to the house, and she would usually stay in this guestroom.) Although to access these spaces, one had to go through a narrow and tall corridor, the light-blue coloring and the natural light beaming from the skylight at the end of the corridor gave this space somewhat of a Mediterranean feel.

In another area, considered to be the climax of the master bedroom and the Villa Savoye, is the skylight which fills the bathroom with natural light. The light shines onto the sink and the bidet is placed there. Yet, the main scene was the dawning of the light onto the mosaic tile clad bathtub and the prototype of the "Chaise Longue" designed Charlotte Perriand[*2]. Also remarkable in this formidable light is the white porcelain tiled walls which stand out from the gray painted round pillars. The forms and colors "polychromy" surrounded by the furniture, the slope adjacent to the pink clad wall, the juxtaposition of the primary colors, and the outlining of the forms become reminiscent of the layout of a Purist painting. Butting up front is the master bedroom and turning right takes one into the boudoir space.

の壁がグレーに塗られた丸柱の柱芯から外れて独立して存在する様も、この自然光により際立たされる。これらのフォルムと色彩（ポリクロミー）の周りには家具を介して廊下側にスロープによって切り取られた壁に彩色されたピンク色など、幾つかの原色がそのフォルムの輪郭と共に重なり合い、まさにピュリスム絵画のようでもある。突き当りが主寝室、右に曲がって前述のブドワがある。

　これら寝室周りでもうひとつ特徴的なのは、家具による空間のアーティキュレーション（分節）であろう。当時、ル・コルビュジエはシャルロット・ペリアンと共に、最小限住宅の設計と共に、多くの規格家具をデザインしていた。この研究成果による家具を、ここではコンクリートでつくった。空間の中にこれらの家具が置かれ、人々はその家具を周り込みながら、書斎やベッドに至るような空間構成が試みられた。

ソラリウムとしての屋上庭園

　2階から3階までのスロープは外部である。手すりも踊場まではコンクリート壁で作られ、踊場では視線を遮るほどの高い壁にいったん囲まれる。折り返すと客船の手すりを思わせるような4本の丸パイプの軽い手すりとなり3階のソラリウムに達する。設計のある段階までは、この3階部分に寝室が計画されていたが、実現したのはソラリウムと回り階段のための階段室だけである。ソラリウムつまり日光浴場と名付けられたこの空間は屋根がなく、壁だけの空間である。

　このソラリウムにはセーヌ川から吹き寄せる風を遮るように北側に、ピュリスム絵画を思わせるような曲面の壁があり、これと連続するような形で階段室が作られている。2階の直方体ヴォリュームからスロープによって抜け出したような、この空間は、まさに客船の甲板の上に出たような感じで周囲を見下ろすことができる。

　スロープを昇りきったところの正面の壁に、セーヌ川まで延びる田園地帯の丘陵を見下ろすことが出来る開口部が空いている。この開口部から切り取られた風景を楽しんだ後、階段室に入り、回り階段を下りてゆく。

Another important feature of the bedroom is the articulation of the space in correspondence to the furniture. At that time, Le Corbusier, along with Charlotte Perriand, designed a lot of the standard furniture to fit along with the minimalist design of the house. The result of their research was realized as furniture that they built in concrete. The furniture was placed in the space where people had to address the space's configuration before being able to reach the study or bed.

Roof Garden as a Solarium

The slope from the 2nd floor to the 3rd floor is placed outside. The handrail, up until the landing, is also made out of the concrete wall, and at the landing the wall becomes higher as if to obstruct the view at this point. Turning around the landing, the handrails that lead one to the "solarium" on the third floor is made of 4 round pipes similar to what you would probably see on a cruise ship. Up to a certain point of the design, a bedroom was designed for this third floor area, but in the end a "solarium" was decided. This space named the "solarium", in other words, the "sunbathing place" is roofless, surrounded by walls on the sides.

At the "solarium", in order to interrupt the blowing winds coming from the Seine River, there is a Purist inspired curvaceous wall on the North side. This space, extended from the rectangular volume of the second floor, feels exactly like the experience of getting off the deck of a cruise ship.

At the end of the slope's descent, one is faced with an opening in the wall that looks onto the pastoral fields that extends all the way to the Seine River. After enjoying this scenery, one continues one's descent by entering the stair shaft and onto the circular staircase.

52

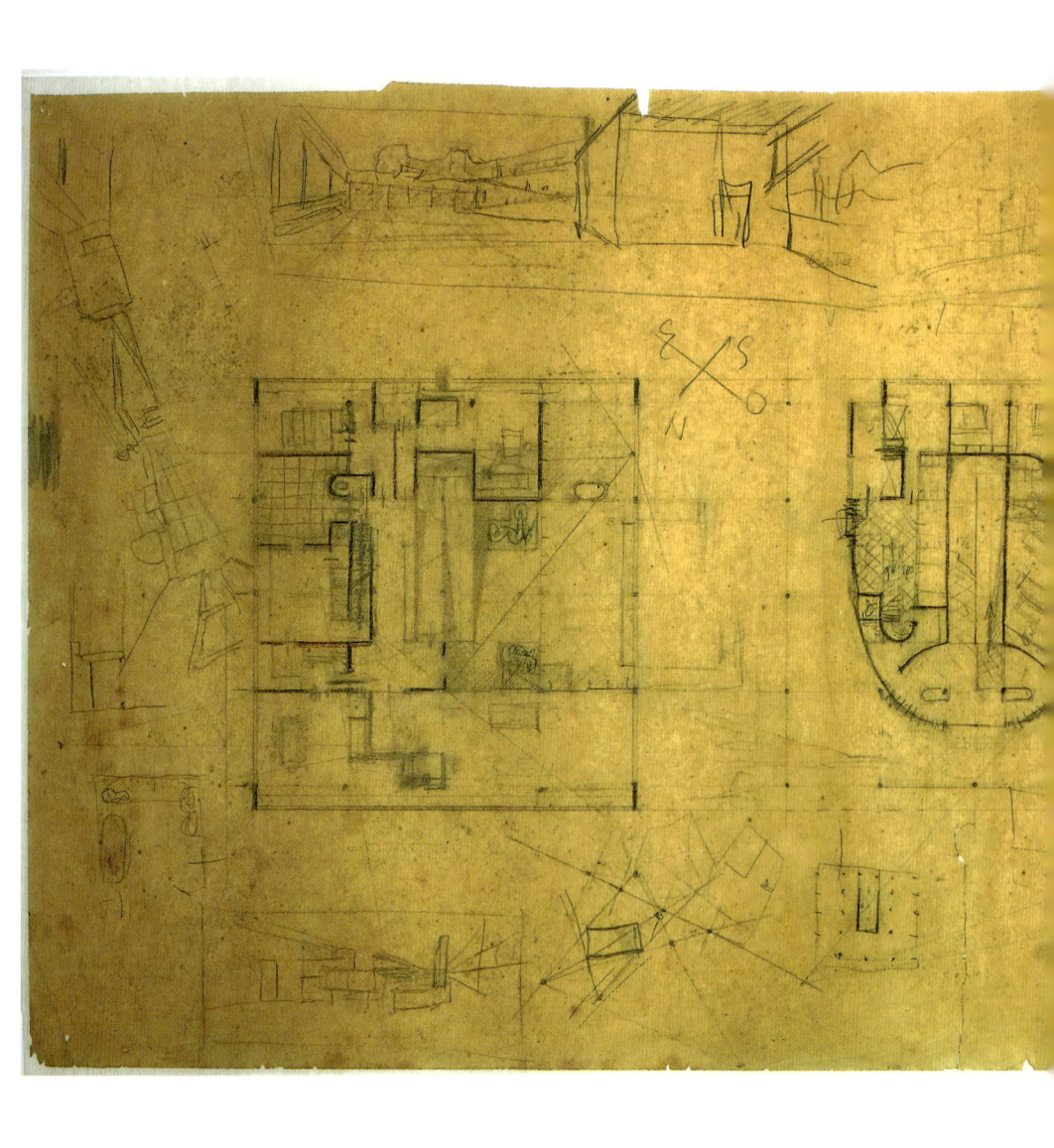

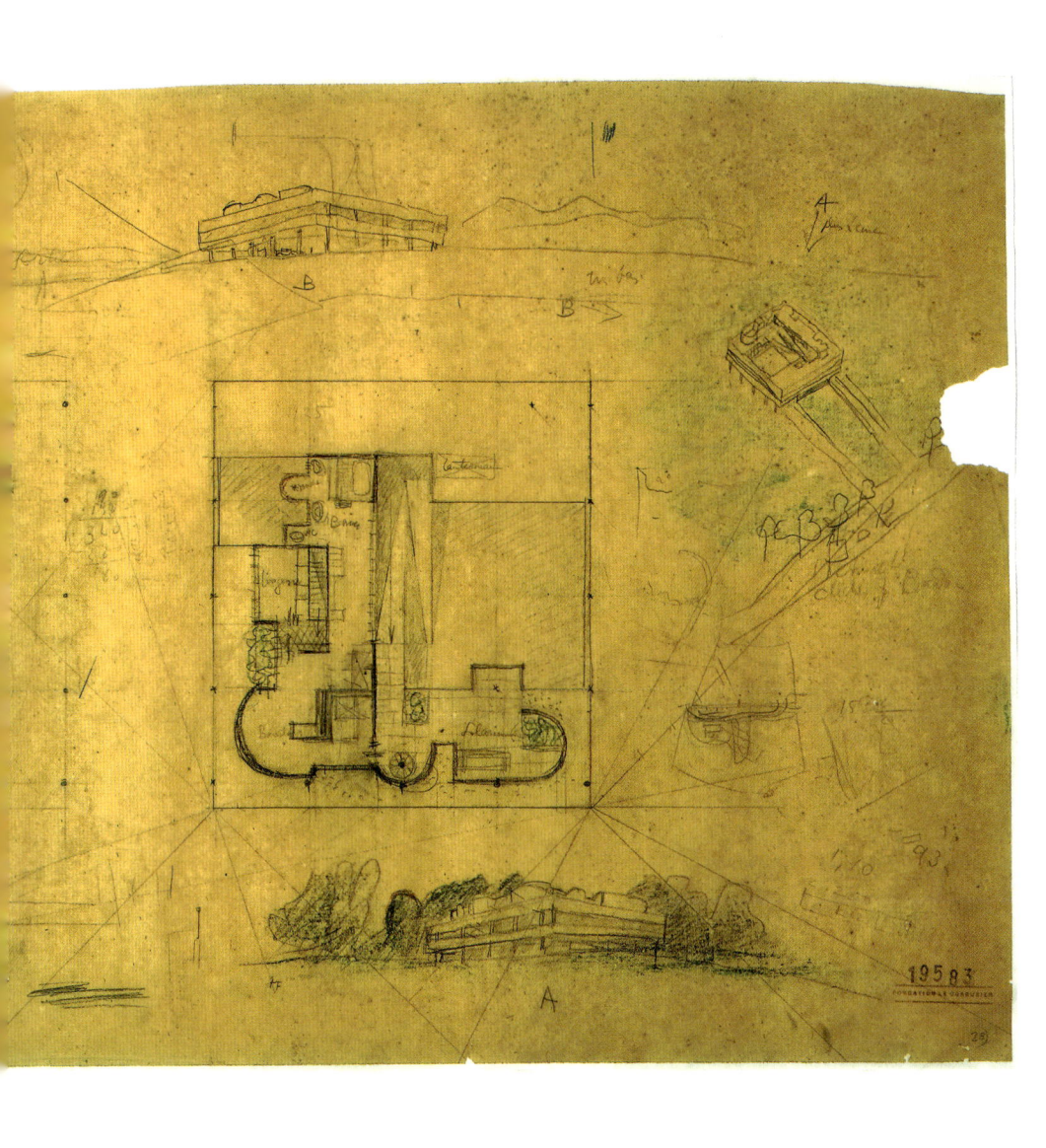

最終設計アイディアをまとめたスケッチ。サヴォア邸のデザイン要素の全てをを読みとることができる。

Sketch summarizing the final design. All of the design elements of the Villa Savoye can be distinguished here.

最もル・コルビュジエらしい作品

　ル・コルビュジエの全作品を概観すると、幾つかのターニングポイントがある。そのなかで、最も重要な時期のひとつに、サヴォア邸竣工の1931年がある。より正確に言うならば、設計の完了した1920年代末かもしれない。

　1917年に再びパリに定住し始め、翌年からピュリストの画家オザンファン[※3]との交流を中心に、パリ美術界に社交の場を拡げる。この頃からサヴォア邸竣工の時期は、抽象絵画であるピュリスム絵画を多く制作するのと同時に、ル・コルビュジエはパリ美術界を中心に拡げた交友から設計依頼を受け、「アトリエ・オザンファン（1922）」「ラ・ロッシュ・ジャンヌレ邸（1923）」「ガルシュの家（1926）」「プラネクス邸（1927）」など、絵画的な「白い住宅」のスケッチを繰り返し実現させていった。

　サヴォア邸設計開始の頃にル・コルビュジエはピュリスム絵画を描くことを辞め、次の段階に移行していった。そして、「白い住宅」の代表作4つを並べ、「建築構成の4つの型」というものをサヴォア邸設計終了時に発表し、サヴォア邸に至る一連の「白い住宅」のまとめを行なう。

[※3]アメデ・オザンファン
画家、批評家。フランス生まれ。
(1886-1966)
ル・コルビュジエとともに、1918年『キュビスム以降』を出版し、ピュリスムを主張した。その後、雑誌「エスプリ・ヌーボー」を創刊する。ル・コルビュジエに、絵画制作、著述活動を始める機会を与えた人物。

Amedee Ozenfant
Painter and critic. Born in France (1886-1966)
"Apres le Cubisme" was published in collaboration with Le Corbusier in 1918, insisting on the Purism movement. Afterwards, the magazine "L'Esprit Nouveau" was launched. Ozenfant was the person who gave Le Corbusier the chance to start his painting career and writing activities.

A Representative Work for Le Corbusier

As one looks at the body of Le Corbusier's works, one could say that there were a few major turning points. And within these turning points, the completion of the Villa Savoye in 1931 would have been one of them. To be more precise, the completion of the design would have probably been towards the end of the 1920's.

　He began his settlement in Paris in 1917, and it was from the following year that he had gotten acquainted with Purist painter Ozenfant[※3], with whom he would go on to expand his social network in the art scene of Paris. It was at that time that Le Corbusier produced many of his Purist paintings, and that he had expanded his social activities to receiving requests for designs, and that was when he realized projects such as Atelier Ozenfant (1922), Maisons La Roche-Jeanneret (1923), Villa Garches (1926), and Maison Planeix (1927), while repeatedly sketching designs for the "White House".

　At the start of the design of the Villa Savoye, Le Corbusier gave up drawing Purist paintings, and shifted his attention to the next stage. Four symbolic works of the "White House" emerged, and Le Corbusier announced what he called the "The Four Compositions of a New Architecture" at the completion of the Villa Savoye.

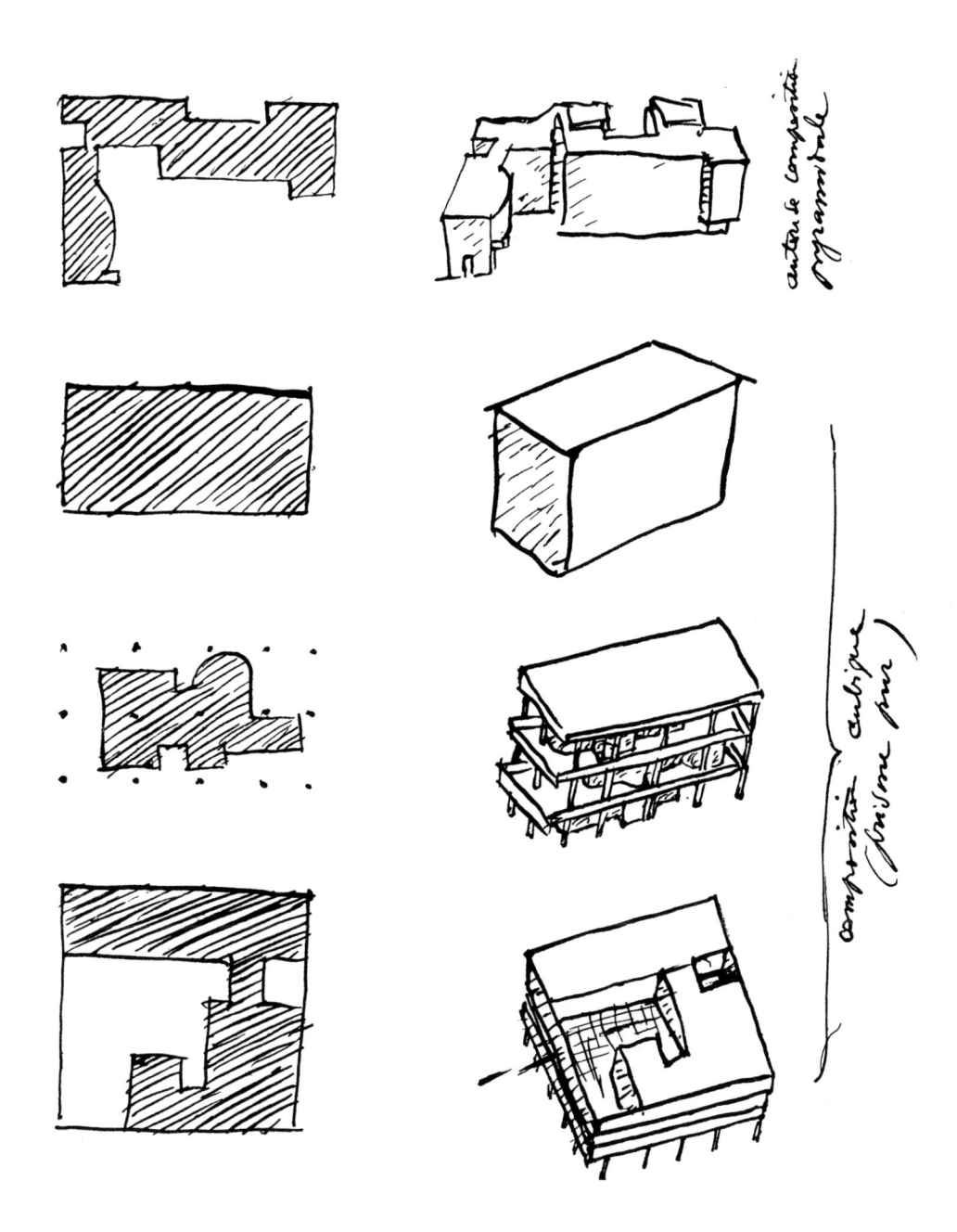

作品中において設計完了時にサヴォア邸と共に紹介された「建築構成の4つの型」。
1920年代に展開された白い住宅の集大成としてサヴォア邸が位置付けられている。
The Villa Savoye was introduced as a compilation of a series of white houses developed in the 1920's as the "The Four Compositions of a New Architecture". The Villa Savoye then took on a reputation of its own.

午前中に絵画を制作し、午後に協同者であった従兄弟のピエール・ジャンヌレと主宰していたセーブル街の設計事務所で設計を行なっていたル・コルビュジエの、「絵画」と「建築」の双方向の抽象的な関係を読み取ることのできる、最もル・コルビュジエらしい時期といえるのかもしれない。その時期の集大成としてサヴォア邸は位置づけられる。

「住む機械」と規格化の美学

　パリでの活動を始めた1920年前後、第一次世界大戦の戦勝国であったフランス国内には、新興の企業家、芸術家が流れ込み、新しい価値観が大きな位置を占めるようになってきていた。その様な人々に向けて、オザンファンと共に出版していたのが雑誌『エスプリ・ヌーヴォー（新しい精神）』[※4]である。ここで、ル・コルビュジエは革命的な言葉「住宅は住む機械」を宣言し、機械（マシン）の大量の図版と共に、その合理性、規格化の美学を主張する。

　1925年のパリ・アール・デコ博覧会で発表する「ヴォワザン計画」のスポンサーになるヴォワザン社も『エスプリ・ヌーヴォー』誌に何度か登場する。この会社は、戦時中の航空機製造契約が解消されるにあたり、住宅産業にのりだすことによって、工場を再活用しようとしていた。

　このように戦争終結による新しい産業構造への転換というチャンスを窺って、ル・コルビュジエは雑誌の発行を通して、新興の企業家たちにメッセージを送っていたとも考えられる。これらの雑誌発表記事をまとめて、ル・コルビュジエは1924年に、20世紀の名著のひとつに数えられる「建築をめざして」を出版する。

[※4]エスプリ・ヌーヴォー
ル・コルビュジエ、オザンファンにダダイストの詩人ポール・デルメを加え、創刊（1920-1924）。

L' Esprit Nouveau
Dadaist's poet Paul Delmet joined Le Corbusier and Ozenfant and launched the publication (1920-1924).

In the mornings, he would spend time to paint, and the afternoons he would be at the office on Sevres Street that he ran with his cousin Pierre Jeanneret. At that time, Le Corbusier was able to develop in both painting and architecture, and that would also be the time when Le Corbusier might have felt the most at his content. The Villa Savoye had come as a compilation of these years of work.

"Machine for Living" and Art of the Standardization

Having began activity in Paris around the 1920's, new entrepreneurs and artists flocked to France after the nation had come back victorious in World War I, and new senses of values were also brought in at that time. With this new audience in mind, Le Corbusier published a new magazine with Ozenfant entitled "L' Esprit Nouveau (new spirit)"[※4]. It was here that Le Corbusier enounced his revolutionary words: "The house is a machine for living", and suggests his ideas of the aesthetics of rationality and standardization with large amounts of illustrations of machines.

Voisin, the company that eventually became the sponsor of the "Voisin plan" and announced in the Paris Art Deco exposition in 1925, appeared several times in the "L' Esprit Nouveau" magazine. This company tried to reuse its factory by entering the housing industry after their aircraft manufacturing contract was canceled during the war.

During this post-war recovery, Le Corbusier had sent a clear message to new entrepreneurs through the issuing of the magazine, encouraging them to look at chances to convert businesses to new industrial establishments. Le Corbusier summarized these writings and publishes one of 20th century's most influential books entitled, "Vers une architecture".

丘の庭に建つサヴォア邸のパース（設計時）。
アンドレア・パラディオのロトンダへの意識がうかがえる。
Perspective of the Villa Savoye on the top of the hill (during design). A consciousness for Andrea Palladio's Villa Rotonda is expressed.

『エスプリ・ヌーヴォー』誌上には、「画一生産の家」「道具としての家」「定型（タイプ）としての家」など、様々な「住む機械」が提案されている。そのなかでも有名なのは1922年のサロンド・ドートンヌで発表した「メゾン・シトロアン」である。ル・コルビュジエがシトロエンという商標に、大量生産のイメージを重ね合わせたことは明白であろう。第一次世界大戦の復興計画のひとつとして構想された集合住宅のために、部品の大量生産を前提に構想された「メゾン・ドミノ」のような具体的な構法システムだけでなく、自動車のような住宅のプロトタイプ、つまり完成形のモデルハウスを示したということにル・コルビュジエのモダニティー（近代性）を感じることができる。

　ル・コルビュジエはサヴォア邸の設計終了直後の1929年10月11日に南米のブエノスアイレスで講演を行なう。そのなかで「サヴォア邸」をアルゼンチンの美しい田園の中にも建てることができることを説く。牛が草を嚙み続けている牧場の、生い茂った草の中に「サヴォア邸」を20戸ほど建て、それぞれの邸宅へ至る道の両側には草が生え、木も花も、牛の群れも自然のままにしておくことができるという、ちゃめっ気いっぱいの説明を、スケッチを描きながら行なった。このことからも判るように、ル・コルビュジエは「今日の」理想的住宅としての「邸宅の定型（タイプ）」、つまりプロトタイプとしてのイメージを、この「サヴォア邸」に強く持ち続けていたことが想像できる。

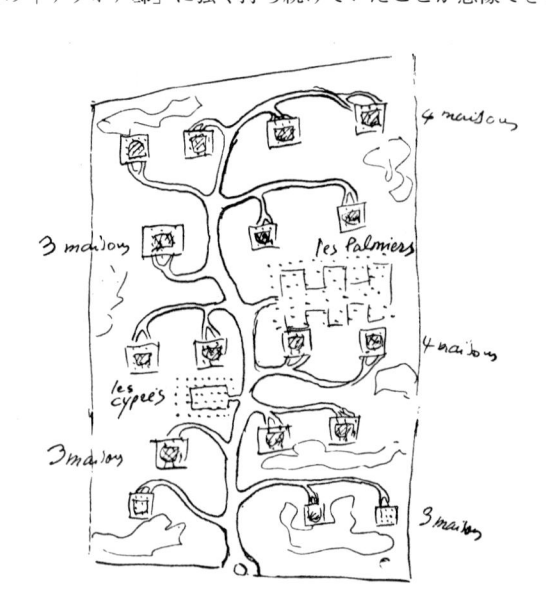

サヴォア邸設計終了時の南米講演の際のスケッチ。
（同右スケッチ）
Sketch of the design of the Villa Savoye while lecturing in South America. (The same right sketch)

Within the L' Esprit Nouveau magazine, various "Living Machines" were proposed, such as "House of uniform production", "House as the tool", and "House as the fixed form (type)". Among those, the most famous is perhaps the "Maison Citrohan" announced at the Salon d' Automn. It was clear that Le Corbusier wanted to make an analogy to mass production manufacturer Citroen. As part of a revival plan after the war, Le Corbusier conceived a building system in which building parts can be manufactured, as concretized in the design of the "Maison Domino". Not only that, but also that the house can also be planned with the development of a prototype model house.

    Le Corbusier gives a lecture in Buenos Aires in South America on October 11th, 1929 immediately after the end of the design of the Villa Savoye. He suggests that the Villa Savoye can be built also in the beautiful country of Argentina. Speaking and sketching at the same time, he explains his proposal of building 20 or so Villa Savoyes in the meadow fields, with roads surrounded by grass, flowers and trees that lead to each house and all across the field, where cows can go about munching on the hay. It is clear that Le Corbusier had a strong image of a "Fixed form of the residence" as the ideal contemporary house, and the Villa Savoye being the prototype for this.

「白の時代」の建築言語

　「住む機械」である住宅の型（タイプ）を、より開かれた形で建築言語としてタイプ化するために、1926年頃、ル・コルビュジエは「①ピロティ、②屋上庭園、③自由な平面、④水平連続窓、⑤自由な立面」という「新しい建築のための五つの点」、いわゆる「近代建築の五原則」をまとめる。そして、1927年の「工作連盟展」におけるシュトゥットガルトのヴァイセンホッフに建設された二棟の住宅と共に、この五原則は発表された。

　ここに出品したミース※5やベーレンス※6などのドイツ工作連盟の建築家と違い、ル・コルビュジエの興味は機械時代の「典型的な人間」の「普遍的な住宅」を作ることであったようだ。工業化、大量生産を目的にしていることは共通であったが、第一機械時代の「人間の新しい精神」に主眼を置いていたことが、ル・コルビュジエの特異性であった。この五原則は「新しい建築」＝「近代建築」を実践しようとする建築家にとって必須の原理となった。この一年後に設計依頼を受けた「サヴォア邸」は、この五原則を最も忠実に明確に表現した典型例となる。

リスキーな施主ピエール・サヴォア

　施主であったピエール・サヴォアは、損害保険会社「ロイズ保険」※7傘下の保険会社「サヴォア保険」のオーナーである。ふたつの大戦間の1931年にサヴォア邸は竣工したが、当時、絵画や文学の分野に限らずビジネスの分野においても、パリは古い価値観と新しい価値観が交錯していた。もちろんル・コルビュジエは新しい価値観の側の人であり、サヴォアさんはその新しい価値観に共鳴して、（実はサヴォア婦人がチャーチ邸を気に入って設計依頼のきっかけになったともいわれている。）週末住宅の設計をル・コルビュジエに依頼したわけである。

　しかし実際は、住人として生活を楽しむこともあったが、漏水をはじめ、住宅を成り立たせる技術の未熟さに苦しめられたとのことである。リスクを判断するのが仕事であったサヴォアさんにして皮肉な話である。

※5 ミース・ファン・デル・ローエ
建築家。ドイツ生まれ。(1886-1969)。"Less is more"（無駄な部分を削ぎ落としたデザインが、より豊かなデザインである）という標語で知られ、インターナショナル・スタイルの成立に貢献した近代建築の巨匠。自由な間取りのユニヴァーサル・スペースという概念を提示し、チューゲンハット邸、ファンズワース邸は今でも住宅の珠玉。

Ludwig Mies van der Rohe
Architect. Born in Germany. (1886-1969). Coined the phrase "Less is more". One of the most influential masterminds of the International Style, he praised the concept of the open "universal space", concretized by works such as the Tugendhat House, and the Farnsworth House.

※7 ロイズ保険
イギリス海軍を後ろ楯に世界的に信用を得ていた、ロンドンに本拠を置く海運・造船の保険を主な事業とする

Lloyd's of London Insurance
With the support of the British naval force, Lloyd's gained worldwide recognition. Being based in London, its major activities consist of insurance for marine transportation and shipbuilding.

The Architectural Lingo of the "White Period"

※6 ペーター・ベーレンス
建築家。ドイツ生まれ。(1868-1940)。ドイツ工作連盟の中心人物。AEGタービン工場（1910年）で 鉄骨造という新しい技術を用いながら、機能優先の工場建築を古典主義的な骨格を持った芸術的なデザインで構成する。ヴァルター・グロピウスやミース・ファン・デル・ローエ、ル・コルビュジエも一時期ベーレンス事務所に在籍していた。モダニズム建築の発展に多大な影響を与えた。

Peter Behrens
Architect. Born in Germany (1868-1940). Kingpin of Deutscher Werkbund. Through the "AEG Turbine Factory", he developed new technologies for iron framework, yet articulating classical designs. Walter Gropius, Mies van der Rohe, and Le Corbusier had all worked at Behrens office for a certain period of time. It had a large influence on the development of the modernist architecture.

To even further transmit the concept of the "Machine for Living" as a typological form of residence, Le Corbusier goes on to identifying the architectural lingo in his so-called doctrines of the "five points of a new architecture", more specifically 1. piloti, 2. roof garden 3. free plan 4. horizontal strip windows, and 5. free façade. Also, in 1927, the five points were announced at the Work Confederation Exhibition in Weissenhof, Stuttgart where 2 houses were built.

Le Corbusier's interest was to make a "Universal house" for the "Typical man" in the age of the machine unlike other architects from the Deutscher Werkbund such as Ludwig Mies van der Rohe[*5] and Peter Behrens[*6] who had exhibited at the event. Aiming at the "Man's new spirit" in the first machine age was Le Corbusier's uniqueness, in the midst in of which it was common to aim towards industrialization and mass production. The five points became indispensable for the architect who tried to practice this mantra of "New architecture" = "Modern architecture". The design for the Villa Savoye which design request mansion which was received the following year represents the classic example abiding to these five principles.

Pierre Savoye, the risky client

Pierre Savoye, was the owner of a subdivision of the insurance company Lloyd's of London[*7], called "Savoye insurance". The Villa Savoye was completed despite two great wars, in a tumultuous era for art and culture, with ripples felt in business, and where old and new senses of values seemed to be at crossroads. Le Corbusier was a person preaching new senses of values, and Savoye resonated to these new philosophies (It is actually believed that the design request was originated by Mrs. Savoye who had seen the Villa Church, and liked it), and that is why Le Corbusier was assigned the design of their weekend getaway.

In reality, although the proprietor had enjoyed a good deal living at the house, certain flaws were detected, such as water leaks here and there, due to the immaturity of the technology of the time. Sarcastically it was risk assessor, Pierre Savoye who actually took the risk to assign the work to Le Corbusier.

第一機械時代の最終章、サヴォア邸

　1931年の新興の「貴族と教養人」。サヴォア夫妻とル・コルビュジエ。この二人がつくりあげた20世紀建築の最高傑作であるポワッシーの「サヴォア邸」。彼らに共通するものは何であったか。それはあるべき「今日の生活」を貪欲にも追い続けたことであったのではないか。今ではル・コルビュジエが当時描いた将来の「今日の生活」は当たり前のものになったが、彼らが持ち続けていた19世紀末以来のポエジー（詩情）、洒落のある生活はどこかに後退してしまった。パリも当時のルミエール（太陽の光）を失いかけているかもしれない。

　ポワッシーの丘にあるサヴォア邸を訪れるたびに、このルミエールによって健全な精神が呼び覚まされる。「今日の建築」はカクアルベキというような、伝統と革新。人間の理性、そしてポエジー。このマニフェストをル・コルビュジエは「透明な時間」と名付けた。サヴォア邸によってポワッシーの丘にある季節の変化を感じ、朝から夕方までの太陽の動きと色を感じる。

　サヴォア邸を散歩する。外側から内側へ。下から上へ、大地から空へ。内側から景色の中へ。これをル・コルビュジエは「プロムナード・アーキテクチュラル」（建築的散策）と呼んだ。太陽の動きの下で建築を散策することによって、そのつど発見される抽象絵画のようなシーンの数々、その連続性。サヴォア邸を設計していたル・コルビュジエはピュリスム絵画の画家として、ピュリスム絵画の最後の1枚を描く意気込みで、3枚の自由な平面にそれぞれ、或いは同時に透明性を追求していたのであろう。

　1920年代をかけて、第一機械時代のヨーロッパの首都パリでデビューを果たしたル・コルビュジエがこの機械時代に別れを告げた記念碑的な作品としてサヴォア邸はある。まさに20世紀の近代性の頂点に位置し、分水嶺を極めた建築作品である。

Villa Savoye, the Last Chapter of the First Age Machine

The new "Aristocrat and lettered man" in 1931. Villa Savoye of Poissy, architectural masterpiece of the 20th century built by The Savoyes and Le Corbusier's. What was common among them? For one, both of them had an avid appetite to chase after the most contemporary lifestyle. Though today, what Le Corbusier had enounced as modern living is pretty much common ground, the chic poetic lifestyle that they had created got somewhat lost in time. Similarly, Paris might also be losing some of its former "lumiere".

An awakening spirit brought in by the so-called "lumiere" fills the guest whenever the Villa Savoye on the hill of Poissy is visited. It is a model for today's architecture, tradition and reform, and an inspiration for man's reason and poetry. Le Corbusier named this manifest the "Transparent time". The changes in the season atop the hill of Poissy where sits the Villa Savoye is felt, and also the changing of the movement and the color of the sun from the morning to the evening is also felt.

Strolling around the Villa Savoye: from the outside to the inside, from bottom to top, and ground to sky, then from the interior to beneath the landscape. This is what Le Corbusier called the "Architectural Promenade". Under the movement of the sun, one shall stroll within the architecture; discover the different scenes as like in an abstract painting in its continuity. With the design of the Villa Savoye, Le Corbusier as a Purist painter painted his final canvas as 3 layered free plans, but each extruding transparency independently.

The 1920's was spent on the design of the Villa Savoye, a monumental work and sort of a bid farewell to the Machine Age for Le Corbusier who had debuted his career in the capital of Europe, Paris during the so called First Machine Age. The Villa Savoye is an architectural masterpiece that stands proudly atop of the podium of modern 20th century architecture.

World Architecture

宮本和義 ©	Photos	© Kazuyoshi Miyamoto
山名善之 ©	Text	© Yoshiyuki Yamana
ヘンリー・ツァン ©	Translation	© Henry Tsang
石原秀一	Chief Editor	Shuichi Ishihara
大石雄一朗	Staff Editor	Yuichiro Oishi
馬嶋正司 ［(株)ポパイ］	Design	Shoji Majima (Popai, Inc.)
川端輝昭 ［(株)ジャパンステージ］	Printer	Teruaki Kawabata (JAPAN STAGE Co.,Ltd.)
松尾茂男	Drawing	Shigeo Matsuo

コルビュジエ財団	Special Thanks	Foundation Le Corbusier
(株)Echelle-1		Echelle-1
(株)カッシーナ・イクスシー		Cassina IXC.Ltd.,
吉川和博		Kazuhiro Yoshikawa

サヴォア邸
1931 フランス
ル・コルビュジエ
2007年7月19日発行

Villa Savoye
1931 France
Le Corbusier
19/7/2007

石原秀一 Publisher Shuichi Ishihara
バナナブックス ©   © Banana Books
〒151-0051東京都渋谷区千駄ヶ谷5-17-15   5-17-15 Sendagaya Shibuya-ku, Tokyo, 151-0051 Japan
TEL.03-5367-6838 FAX.03-5367-4635   Tel.+81-3-5367-6838 Fax.+81-3-5367-4635
URL: http://bananabooks.cc/   URL: http://bananabooks.cc/

BANANA BOOKS
PRINTED IN JAPAN
ISBN978-4-902930-12-2 C3352
©FLC/ADAGP, Paris&SPDA, Tokyo, 2007

禁無断転載
落丁・乱丁本はおとりかえします。